Text copyright © 2000 by Black Dog & Leventhal Publishers, Inc.
Illustrations copyright © 2000 by Rick Peterson

Published by
Black Dog & Leventhal Publishers, Inc.
151 West 19th Street
New York, NY 10011

Distributed by
Workman Publishing Company
225 Varick Street
New York, NY 10014

Designed by 27.12 design, ltd.

Manufactured in China

h g f e

Library-of-Congress Cataloging-in-Publication Data

Bruun, Erik A., 1961-
Virginia / by Erik Bruun.
p. cm. -- (State Shapes)

Summary: Presents the history, important people, and famous places of the
Old Dominion state, as well as miscellaneous facts about Virginia today.

ISBN-13:978-1-57912-103-7
1. Virginia--Juvenile literature. [1. Virginia.] I. Title.

F226.3 .B78 2000

975.5--dc21   00-024670

VIRGINIA

By ERIK BRUUN

illustrated by

RICK PETERSON

BLACK DOG
& LEVENTHAL
PUBLISHERS
NEW YORK

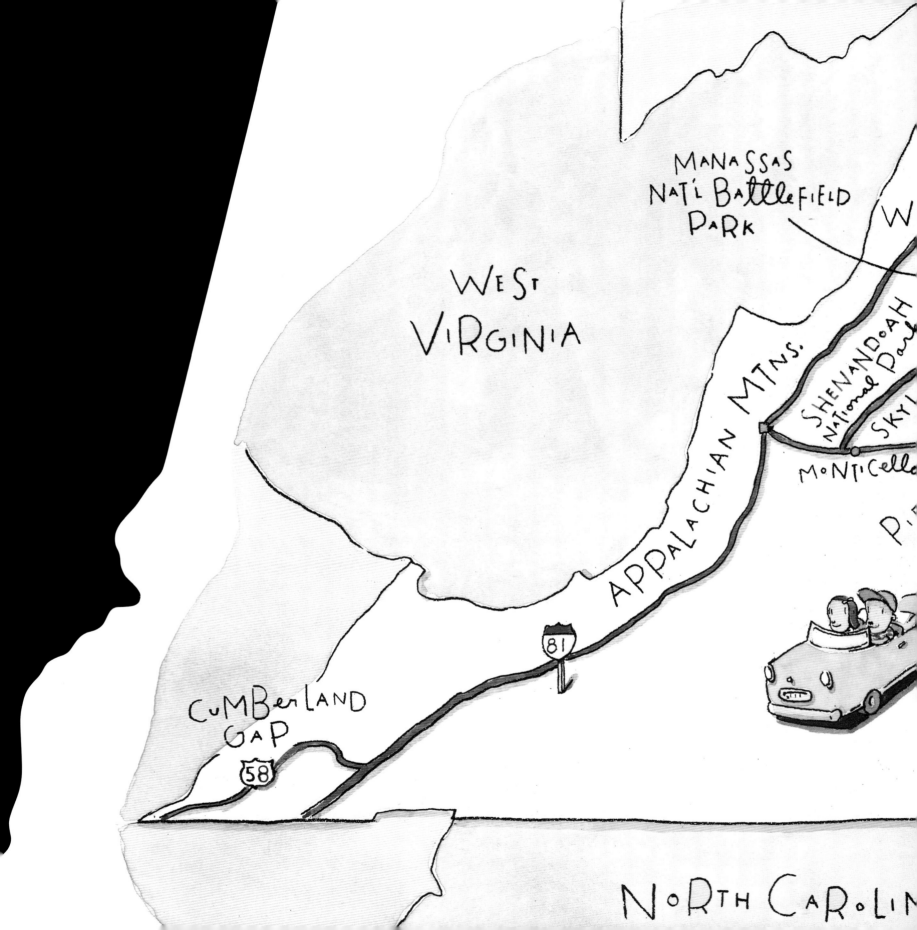

MANASSAS
NAT'L BATTLEFIELD
PARK

W

WEST
VIRGINIA

APPALACHIAN MTNS.

SHENANDOAH
National Park

SKYL

MONTICELLO

P

81

CUMBERLAND
GAP

58

NORTH CAROLIN

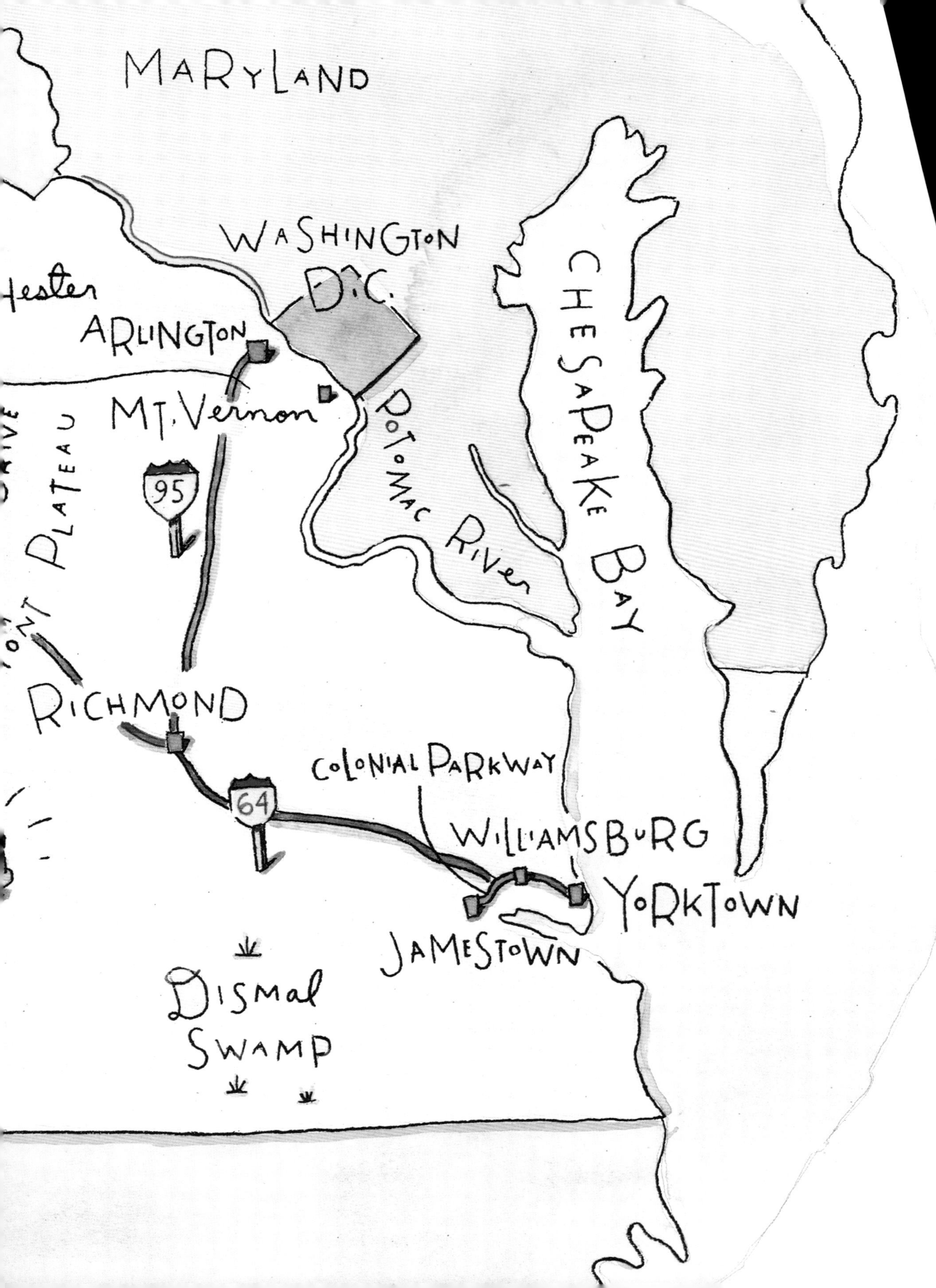
MARYLAND
WASHINGTON
D.C.
ARLINGTON
MT. Vernon
95
PLATEAU
POTOMAC River
CHESAPEAKE BAY
RICHMOND
64
COLONIAL PARKWAY
WILLIAMSBURG
YORKTOWN
JAMESTOWN
Dismal
SWAMP

Welcome to Virginia! My name is Beauregard T. Jackson, but you can call me Beau. It will be my honor to take you on a tour through the great historic state of Virginia—home of our nation's founding fathers, birthplace of eight presidents and the fiercest battleground of that great conflict known as the American Civil War. It's a big state—39,598 square miles, to be exact! But don't worry too much about numbers. This won't be like school. It will be fun!

39,598 Sq. miles

THE STORY of the UNITED STATES BEGINS IN VIRGINIA.

GIVE ME LIBERTY

Q. All American foxhounds (the state animal of Virginia) are descendants of dogs owned by which president?

Sounds great, Beau.
My name is Penny and
this is my dog, Skipper.
We can't wait to start.
I hope we'll see some battlefields!

Sounds like you are a young woman with an appreciation for history, Penny. Yes, we will view the fields of war that shaped our nation. But there will be much more. You will see magnificent sights, from the Chesapeake Bay in the east to Shenandoah Valley's deep-green fields and the magnificent Blue Ridge Mountains in western Virginia.

You will learn about men and women who helped make our nation great. You will read stories of tragedy and humor. You will learn facts small and large. Virginia is not just about the grand parade of history. It is a tale of men, women and children just like you, who struggled to do the right thing, the best way they could.

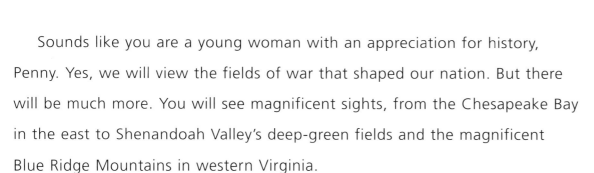

 George Washington. Washington was a Virginian, himself, and he bred the dogs for hunting. They are one of only four breeds to originate in the United States.

the TIDEWATER

*O*ur trip starts in Jamestown, site of the first permanent British settlement in North America. Today, you can see the archeological remains of the original site and a reconstructed village that looks much like it did 350 years ago.

Jamestown is on the James River. The eastern third of Virginia is called the Tidewater. Rivers and inlets make this a beautiful area with wide beaches along the Atlantic Ocean. Many sections are covered with swamps. The biggest swamp of all is The Great Dismal Swamp in southern Virginia.

A "dismal" swamp doesn't sound so great to me.

It is anything *but* dismal. The first settlers called it "dismal" because they couldn't build anything there—and because of all the snakes!

Q. What did the British sea captain Sir Francis Drake originally call Virginia when he claimed it for England in the 1570s?

But it has so many other types of plants and animals that George Washington called it "a glorious paradise." It is now a 107,000-acre national wildlife refuge. There are more than 200 species of birds, incredible forests and stunningly beautiful flowers.

So, was Jamestown near a swamp?

The settlement was further north than the Dismal Swamp, but there was indeed swampland in the area near Jamestown, and that was a big problem. In the first ten years, six out of seven of the original settlers died. When the first ones arrived in 1607, they were looking for gold and a "northwest passage" to Asia. They didn't find either, just misery. Most were the sons of the wealthy and privileged looking for adventure. Unfortunately, they didn't know anything about starting a colony. Some settlers refused to work, saying they were noblemen. Being near a swamp made it much easier for them to catch diseases and die.

 New Albion. "Albion" is the Latin word for England.

Native Americans from the Powhatan Confederacy lived along the coast. They grew fields of corn around their villages. When the British arrived, the Native Americans were suspicious. Other Europeans had raided the Virginia coast to kidnap them as slaves. Pocahontas was the daughter of a powerful chief. Her name meant "the playful one." According to legend, Pocahontas helped bring peace between the Jamestown settlers and her Algonquin tribe by stopping her father from executing Jamestown's leader, John Smith. (Some historians doubt this actually happened.) Smith was a strong leader and one tough pioneer. He told the others that if they didn't work, they wouldn't get food. He traded with the local villages for corn. When Smith returned to England after two years, Jamestown once again suffered.

Disagreements between Jamestown and local Native Americans led to fights. In the winter of 1609-10, Native Americans wouldn't let settlers out of

Q. What's Virginia's state song?

10

Jamestown. This was called "The Starving Time." Out of 500 settlers, only 60 survived the winter. But new pioneers kept arriving, so the settlement got another chance.

What happened to Pocahontas?

She fell in love with a settler named John Rolfe. When they married, the fighting stopped. This was called the "Pocahontas Peace." They had a son and traveled to England, where Pocahontas died of smallpox at the age of 21. Because Native Americans had never been exposed to smallpox, the disease killed thousands of them.

JOHN ROLFE AND POCAHONTAS

 "Carry Me Back to Old Virginia" written by James Bland, one of the greatest African-American writers of folk songs.

ALL IN FAVOR?

Terrible battles later took place between the Native Americans and the colonists, but when Rolfe started to grow the Native American crop tobacco in 1614, Jamestown became a very profitable place. It was still a hard life, but soon more towns were settled, and Virginia started to flourish. In 1619, the first democratically elected assembly, the House of Burgess, met in Jamestown.

the House of Burgess

What's this Colonial Parkway, Beau? Is that how the settlers moved around?

The Colonial Parkway is the modern road that takes us through the "Colonial Triangle" to Williamsburg and Yorktown. The settlers didn't use many roads, because in those days cars hadn't been invented. Instead, people often traveled by boat. Virginia's wide, slow-moving rivers made it easy for ships to go

Q. When was the first Thanksgiving celebrated?

deep into the countryside. Plantations were built along rivers the same way houses are built along roads today. By the end of the 1600s, Virginia had 50,000 settlers, more than any other British colony.

Many of the settlers planted tobacco. Growing it required a lot of land and a lot of hard work, so planters imported slaves from Africa to work the fields. The first Africans arrived in 1619 as "indentured servants" who had to work for a certain person for several years, but were then freed. Many of the first Africans became freemen. Over the next fifty years, however, a wealthy class of planters had emerged who needed slaves to work their plantations. They passed laws that allowed them to treat African-Americans more like property than people. Slaves were bought and sold like cattle.

That's terrible.

You're right, Penny, it was, but we'll see later how slavery came to an end.

 Virginia claims to have celebrated the first Thanksgiving in 1619, when a local leader wrote that December 4 would be celebrated "yearly. . . as a day of Thanksgiving." This was later changed to the last Thursday in November.

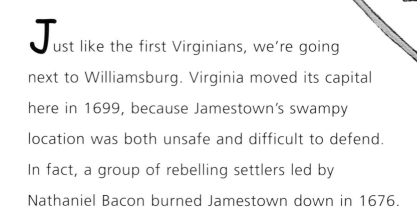

Just like the first Virginians, we're going next to Williamsburg. Virginia moved its capital here in 1699, because Jamestown's swampy location was both unsafe and difficult to defend. In fact, a group of rebelling settlers led by Nathaniel Bacon burned Jamestown down in 1676.

Why is everybody in Williamsburg dressed in clothes from colonial times?

Williamsburg is a living museum. More than 500 buildings have been restored to preserve Colonial Williamsburg as a community complete with actors who dress, speak and pretend to live just as they did 250 years ago. It's hard to believe now, but Williamsburg 75 years ago was a rundown village. A local historian convinced John D. Rockefeller, Jr., to invest millions of dollars to restore Williamsburg to its former glory.

Q. What is the most popular historic tourist attraction in the United States?

But what made

Williamsburg so special?

It was the capital and commercial center for most of the 1700s. Thomas Jefferson, George Washington, Patrick Henry and many of the nation's founders lived, studied and worked in Williamsburg, which is also the location of William and Mary College, the oldest college in the United States.

When the American colonists contemplated declaring independence from England in the 1770s, men like Patrick Henry frequently met in Williamsburg to debate whether the colonies should rebel against the British. Patrick Henry is famous for his speech that declared, "Give me liberty or give me death!"

Jefferson moved the capital again to Richmond in 1780, because the town couldn't be defended from advancing British soldiers. Those soldiers, however, were soon trapped by Washington and his army at Yorktown, which is our next stop.

A. Colonial Williamsburg. Even more popular, though, are the nearby theme amusement parks, Busch Gardens and Water Country USA.

15

The American Revolution ended here, in Yorktown. Virginians played a major role in the Revolution. George Washington commanded the Continental Army; Thomas Jefferson wrote the Declaration of Independence in 1776; and thousands of men and boys from Virginia fought in the army. In 1781, Washington trapped the British army in Yorktown, a busy port for the local tobacco plantations. When ships from the French navy arrived to cut off the British from reinforcements, the British surrendered. America had won the Revolutionary War.

Way to go, Virginia!

Q. What city is home to the largest Arby's in the world?

JAMES MONROE

GEORGE WASHINGTON

JAMES MADISON

But Virginia's contribution to the founding of the United States didn't stop there. Four out of the first five presidents—Washington, Jefferson, James Madison and James Monroe—came from Virginia. In all, eight presidents were Virginians, more than from any other state. The others were William Henry Harrison, John Tyler, Zachary Taylor and Woodrow Wilson. That's why Virginia is sometimes called the "Mother of Presidents."

THOMAS JEFFERSON

Virginia was a huge state back then. Not only did it have more people than any other state, it was also by far the largest. At the time of the American Revolution, Virginia claimed to own much of the land that is now Kentucky, West Virginia, Illinois, Indiana, Michigan, Minnesota, Ohio and Wisconsin. Hence the origin of another Virginia nickname: Mother of States. Because other states were worried that Virginia might get too bossy, Virginia gave up its claim for land in the West.

 Colonial Heights, Virginia. It features a totem pole, cathedral ceilings, a fireplace, fancy chairs and carpets, and a special menu.

In exchange for giving up its land claims, Virginia wanted the nation's capital nearby. The state (and Maryland) donated land to the federal government on the Potomac River in northern Virginia. This became Washington, D. C., which stands for District of Columbia. It was named after George Washington, the nation's first president.

He sure did a lot.

Washington played such an important role in starting the United States that he is known as the "Father of His Country." For eight years during the American Revolution, he led his troops in the face of starvation, defeats on the battlefield and other terrible hardships.

Washington's leadership kept the army together. When the war ended, Americans begged him to lead the new government. He became president in 1789. If it had not been for Washington, the world's first modern democratic government could have easily failed. And the whole time, he just wanted to return to his home

 Q. What is the state bird of Virginia?

MOUNT VERNON

at nearby Mount Vernon. "No estate is more pleasantly situated than this," Washington wrote of his 8,000-acre property.

Washington ran five separate farms at Mount Vernon. Almost all of the food, equipment and tools were grown in its fields, forged in its blacksmith shop or manufactured on site. Washington even "farmed" the Potomac River for fish each spring. One year, his slaves caught more than a million fish in six weeks. Mount Vernon helped make Washington one of the wealthiest men of his time. Both he and his wife, Martha, are buried there. It is still a beautiful house to visit.

 A. The cardinal. In early times it was called the Virginia nightingale.

There sure are a lot of rivers in Virginia.

Yes, Penny, there are, and 48 of Virginia's rivers drain into the Chesapeake Bay. The Potomac is among the most famous. When the British first arrived, the river was so thick with fish that John Smith declared that, "for want of nets, we attempted to catch them with frying pans."

In the 1700s, fishermen from Maryland and Virginia fought over who could use different sides of the river to gather oysters. The feud, known as "The Oyster Wars," was a perfect example of why the country needed to form a strong national government to resolve disputes between the states.

A war? I guess oysters must have been pretty important!

Q. Where in Virginia can you still find wild horses?

I'M A VIRGINIAN.

Native Americans and colonists living around the Chesapeake relied very heavily on oysters for food. Chesapeake Bay comes from the Algonquin Indian word meaning "great shellfish bay." More than 100 million pounds of crabs and half the nation's clams are still pulled from the Chesapeake each year. The writer H. L. Mencken described the bay as an "immense protein factory" due to all the fish, oysters, crabs and shellfish. Plus, more than 1 million ducks, geese and other waterfowl live on the bay.

The 74,000-square-mile Chesapeake is the country's largest bay. The shoreline, which also borders Maryland, is 4,000 miles long—longer than the distance across the mainland United States from the Pacific to the Atlantic Oceans. Delmarva is a coastal region on the eastern side of the Chesapeake that got its name from the three states are parts of it—*Del*aware, *Mar*yland and *Virginia*.

A. On Assateague Island near the Delmarva peninsula. The island is a beautiful national wildlife refuge and is home to herds of wild horses.

What's that big, funny-shaped building?

That's the Pentagon, headquarters of the United States Armed Forces. It is the biggest office building in the world, with 6.5 million square feet of space, 4,200 clocks, 691 water fountains and 284 restrooms. "Pentagon" means "five sides," which is the shape of the building.

I bet lots of people work there.

This whole area from Washington, D.C. south to Richmond is swarming with people who work for the federal government— 500,000 Virginians work on the federal payroll. Virginia also has several military bases. The Norfolk Naval Base in southeastern Virginia is one of the largest navy yards in the world, and the Marines have an important training center at Quantico on the Potomac.

Q. How is Tangier Island, off the Delmarva peninsula, like a different country?

But not all Virginians work for the government. Virginia companies make chemicals, clothing, furniture, paper and cigarettes. The state government has been very active in promoting business. Virginia used to be among the poorest states, but it's now one of the fastest growing. Many companies have opened new factories. Shipbuilding has always been big in Virginia, especially the shipyards at Newport News and Portsmouth. Coal mining is huge in western Virginia. Giant

machines remove coal from open strip-mining pits. Norfolk is the largest coal-exporting port in the nation.

A. In addition to owning no cars, the residents of Tangier Island claim their own version and pronunciation of the English language.

TOMB of the UNKNOWN SOLDIER

What about that beautiful cemetery?
It looks important.

That is sacred ground, Penny. It is Arlington National Cemetery, the final resting place of more than 200,000 American soldiers, heroes and public figures. Row after row of plain, white headstones mark the graves of men and women who fought and died for their country. The Tomb of the Unknown Soldier is here, as well as the eternal flame marking the grave of President John F. Kennedy. This solemn piece of land was once owned by Robert E. Lee, but it was turned into a cemetery for Union soldiers in 1864.

Q. What was the first toll road in the United States?

That name sounds familiar. Who was Robert E. Lee?

Who was Robert E. Lee? He was a general for the Confederacy during the Civil War who was beloved by southerners and respected by the entire nation. In fact, he was offered the position of head of the Union army, but turned it down to lead the South. General Lee commanded the Army of Northern Virginia Army and won great victories against the Union, pushing the Yankee army back from Richmond in 1862, and then defeating them time and again despite being outnumbered. But Lee was more than a general. He was a great man. When southerners talk about chivalry and honor, Lee is the role model. He was one of this country's toughest soldiers, but he never cursed. Lee opposed slavery, but he fought to defend his state. He ordered his men into battle, but his soldiers loved him: They refused to let him on the front line for fear of his being killed.

So is this where the Civil War battlefields are?

No, there wasn't much fighting around Washington, D. C. Let's head to Richmond—there are some amazing battlefields along the way.

 A. The Little River Turnpike, connecting Alexandria just south of Washington, D. C., to Snicker's Gap. It was built in the late 1700s.

I'm confused, Beau. If Virginia was so important in starting the United States, how come Virginia fought against the U. S. government in the Civil War?

Very good question. Like almost all of the states in the 1700s, Virginia was a slave state. But after the American Revolution, the northern states abolished slavery because they thought it was wrong for one person to own another. In the South, the need for slaves in a plantation economy and a genuine belief that whites were superior outweighed other considerations, and slavery remained legal.

In Virginia, slaves sometimes tried to run away or to rebel against their owners. The most famous rebellion was led by a slave named Nat Turner. In the 1830s, Virginia almost voted to abolish slavery, but many whites were afraid slaves would try to kill them. Instead, they made even stricter laws, making it illegal for slaves to read, travel without permission, or even gather in groups without a white person present.

Q. Why did West Virginia break off from the rest of the state?

That doesn't sound very democratic to me.

It wasn't. But the whites in Virginia were in a difficult situation. Slaves and farming were their main source of wealth. Virginia had once been the biggest, grandest state, and it was starting to lose its influence. States like New York and Massachusetts had built factories and were booming. When Abraham Lincoln was elected president in 1860, whites in southern states were afraid the national government would force their states to abolish slavery. They didn't think the national government should be able tell the states what to do. Some of the states, including Virginia, voted to form a new country called the Confederate States of America. Lincoln wouldn't let the South leave, though, and soon war broke out.

A. When Virginia voted to join the Confederacy, most people in western Virginia didn't own slaves, so they voted to leave Virginia, form their own state (West Virginia) and join the North.

When Virginia joined the Confederacy, the South decided to make Richmond its capital. From 1861 to 1865 the armies of the North and South fought some of the fiercest battles of the war as each side tried to capture the other's capital. More battles were fought in Virginia than in any other state. In some battles, more Americans were killed in a single day than in the entire American Revolution. Today, many of the battlefields are national parks. Manassas National Battlefield Park was the site of two major battles.

Today it's so beautiful and peaceful.
    It's hard to imagine thousands of men killing each other here.

Q. Where was Jackson buried?

The First Battle of Manassas, or Bull Run, was the first major battle of the war. It was a terrible shock to the soldiers and the country to have Americans killing Americans. This was where my great-great-great-great granduncle General Thomas Jackson earned his nickname "Stonewall." As other Confederate soldiers fled the field, a general called out: "There stands Jackson like a stone wall. Rally behind the Virginians!" One year later, Jackson helped Lee win one of his greatest victories at the Second Battle of Manassas. Some of the other national parks commemorate battles at Fredericksburg, Spotsylvania, Petersburg and Appomattox Courthouse, where General Lee surrendered. And then there is Chancellorsville where Jackson was accidentally shot in the arm after the battle by one of his own soldiers. He died shortly afterward.

 A. He was buried in two cemeteries. His arm, which was amputated, is buried at Chancellorsville. The rest of his body lies in Lexington.

THE STATE CAPITAL IN RICHMOND

We are now in Richmond—state capital of Virginia since 1780, capital of the Confederacy during the Civil War, and to old-time southerners, who consider it the center of just about everything, "the navel of the universe."

It's one busy belly button!

It sure is. Anyone coming to Richmond expecting a sleepy city decorated with old-fashioned mansions is in for a surprise. It is a bustling place. First, you can see our rich history. Thomas Jefferson designed the Capitol building to house the state legislature, the oldest in the nation. During the Civil War it was not only the center of the government, but a huge military headquarters, with thousands and thousands of soldiers as well as hospitals, prison camps and supply centers. You can see what Richmond used to be like by visiting the White House of the Confederacy.

Q. Why does the 900 block of Terminal Place in Richmond smell so good?

But it's not white, Beau, it's gray!

Well, gray was the color of the Confederate soldiers' uniforms. Richmond is also home to the Museum of the Confederacy, which holds the largest collection of Civil War memorabilia. There is also the Valentine Museum, which explores our social history.

When the Yankees finally took Richmond at the very end of the war, fire destroyed the city. Richmond, and almost all of Virginia, had to be rebuilt nearly from scratch. The state was so poor at that time that it had to close half its schools. It took thirty years before the economy started to recover in earnest with iron mills, tobacco and textile factories.

Richmond today is a major center for international businesses. Plus, it's the only city where you can go whitewater rafting downtown.

 A. Because over one million pounds of cookies are produced there every week!

MaGGie Walker

Richmond was also the home to some famous and important people, particularly African Americans. Arthur Ashe grew up and took tennis lessons in Richmond. He later became the first black man to win Wimbledon, helping break down racial barriers in sports. Bill "Bojangles" Robinson was considered one of the greatest tap dancers in our history.

Then there was Maggie Walker who worked her way up to become the first African-American woman in the United States to be a bank president. The daughter of a kitchen slave, she took over a small organization that pooled people's money to take care of the sick and in 1903 turned the organization into the St. Luke Penny Savings Bank. It became Richmond's largest bank for African Americans.

So things were much better for
African Americans after slavery ended.

Q. Who had the fastest feet in Richmond?

Yes, but it's taken a long time and it hasn't been smooth or easy. A lot of white Virginians didn't want to give the blacks freedom or equality. They passed laws making it illegal for blacks to share

MARCHING for CIVIL RIGHTS

services, like drinking from the same water fountain or going to the same schools.

Whites called it separate but equal, but most blacks didn't think so. It wasn't until the civil rights movement of the 1950s and 1960s that the laws were changed. It's taken even longer to change people's attitudes. But in 1989, Virginia elected Douglas Wilder as governor, the first African-American governor in the United States. It was a great sign that change is possible.

A. Bill "Bojangles" Robinson. He once held the world record for running backward, going 75 yards in 8.2 seconds.

the PIEDMONT PLATEAU

This part of Virginia seems different. It's not as flat.

You have a keen eye, Penny. We are on the edge of the Piedmont Plateau, which stretches across the center of Virginia. Many rivers, streams and brooks crisscross the Piedmont's hilly fields and forests. The rich soil here has helped make the Piedmont area a very important farming center. Virginia's horse country in central Virginia, with its beautiful, rolling estates, is one of the richest and most beautiful places in the nation.

When you fly over the countryside, the Piedmont Plateau looks like a patchwork of farms. Tobacco is still the most important crop, but Virginia farms also grow wheat, corn and soybeans. Virginia is also one of the leading states for raising beef, turkeys and chickens.

Q. Why does Texas owe much of its heritage to Virginia?

34

Don't forget
　　　　the Virginia hams!

All told, there are more than 40,000 farms. The average size of each farm is almost the same as 200 football fields. Almost all of the farms are still owned by families. Of course, there used to be a lot more Virginians who worked in the countryside on farms. A lot of them have moved to the cities, especially around Washington, D.C., and Richmond. Half of all Virginians now live in that area, because that's where the growth and opportunities are. In fact, I bet you didn't know that the number of people in Virginia has more than doubled since 1950 to 6.8 million people in 2000. Virginia may not be the largest state anymore, but it's still one of the big ones!

RICHMOND

 Sam Houston and Stephen F. Austin, legendary heroes of Texas history, both came from Virginia. They were some of Texas's original founding fathers, and both Virginians have cities named after them in Texas.

This place looks familiar.

It should. Pull out a nickel, and look at the back.

Wow! It's the same building!

This is Monticello, Thomas Jefferson's home. Jefferson spent forty years designing, building and refining Monticello. The 21-room mansion and plantation on a hilltop is considered among the most beautiful properties in the United States. It still holds Jefferson's telescope, 7,000-book library and furniture—some of which he designed himself.

Jefferson had his eccentricities. He didn't like staircases, so the staircases at Monticello are hidden and narrow. He invented all sorts of odd things, like a seven-day clock and an indoor compass, which showed him from which direction the wind was blowing outside.

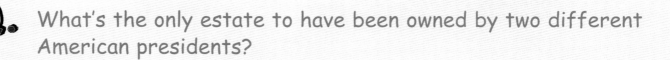

Q. What's the only estate to have been owned by two different American presidents?

36

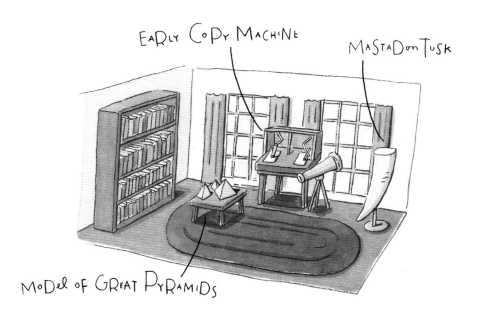

EARLY COPY MACHINE

MASTADON TUSK

MODEL OF GREAT PYRAMIDS

And he loved to garden. Jefferson cultivated over 250 different types of vegetables (peas were one of his favorites) and 170 different types of fruit on a terrace that was 1,000 feet wide. "The greatest service which can be rendered to any country is to add a useful plant to its culture," Jefferson wrote.

But he wasn't perfect. Although Jefferson wrote the Declaration of Independence, proclaiming that all men are created equal, Jefferson had 130 slaves who ran Monticello. It is one of the great ironies of American history. Jefferson—who did so much to establish freedoms for Americans—could never bring himself to free his own slaves, even though he knew it was wrong.

A. The homestead of Sherwood Forest in Virginia. It was owned by Presidents William Henry Harrison and John Tyler.

But didn't Jefferson do other things, too?

Oh, I almost forgot—he was the third President of the United States. He wasn't your ordinary run-of-the-mill president either. For starters, he was the first president who was not a Federalist, which was the political party that had led the nation up until then. That may not sound like a big deal today, but back then it was. People worried that Jefferson might throw his political enemies in the Federalist party in jail when he became president. But he didn't. This meant that Americans could really be free to disagree with the government without fear of being punished.

Then, of course, he doubled the size of the country with the Louisiana Purchase in 1803. For $15 million—or the yearly salary of a really good Major League baseball pitcher—Jefferson bought from France more than 800,000 square miles, from Louisiana north all the way to Minnesota and west to the edge of the Rocky Mountains. Jefferson sent two other Virginians, Meriwether Lewis and William Clark, on their famous journey across the continent to

PRESIDENT, LANDSCAPER, ARCHITECT...

Q. Which president served the shortest term in office?

LEWIS and CLARK

the Pacific Ocean. Lewis and Clark (and 49 others) spent two years traveling more than 8,000 miles to officially explore the West for the first time.

Jefferson's keen mind influenced other important leaders, such as Presidents James Madison and James Monroe, whose historic estate Ash Lawn-Highland is a few miles away from Monticello. Because of his deep love of philosophy and education, Jefferson founded and designed the University of Virginia in nearby Charlottesville. To this day, it is one of the most beautiful and prestigious universities in the nation.

THE UNIVERSITY of VIRGINIA

A. William Henry Harrison of Virginia. He caught a cold while delivering his inaugural address and died exactly one month later of pneumonia.

the APPALACHIAN MOUNTAINS

Time to head west into the Appalachian mountains, which cover the western third of Virginia. The Blue Ridge Mountains run along the western edge of the Piedmont. This is where Virginia's highest mountains are, towering above the Piedmont region to the east and the Shenandoah Valley to the west.

The views are beautiful!

More than a million people visit the Shenandoah National Park along the top of the Blue Ridge Mountains each year. They have built a scenic road, the 105-mile-long Skyline Drive, where you can enjoy the view while traveling. Away from the road, the National Park Service has let the region grow wild. Its forested mountainsides now include bear, bobcat, turkey and more than 200 different types of birds. It's a beautiful place to go hiking, biking, camping, fishing—some people even go hang-gliding!

Q. How is Richmond unlike every other major metropolitan area in the US?

Brrr! It's colder up here.

Anyone who thinks Virginia is just sun and warmth hasn't spent time in the mountains. Snow may stay on the ground for months in the wintertime up here. As we head farther west, Virginia gets even more rugged, with steep mountains, plunging waterfalls, cliffs and deep ravines. A lot of people don't realize it, but there's snow skiing in Virginia. The record low temperature was minus 29 degrees Fahrenheit at Monterey on February 10, 1899. Of course, it also gets pretty darn hot in Virginia, too. The record high temperature was 110 degrees Fahrenheit at Columbia on July 5, 1954. That's just about hot enough to fry an egg!

-29°F FEB. 10, 1899

110°F JULY 5, 1954

 A. You can go rafting right through the heart of the city. Richmond Raft Company offers an "urban whitewater" experience along the James River in downtown Richmond.

Down into the Shenandoah Valley we go. There are so many farms here that it was called "the breadbasket of the Confederacy" during the Civil War. Union and Confederate armies fought back and forth for the Shenandoah Valley so often that one town, Winchester, changed hands more than 70 times. Stonewall Jackson made military history in the Shenandoah when he and 8,000 soldiers outfought and outwitted three larger Union armies in his famous Valley Campaign of 1862. Both Jackson and Lee are buried at Lexington in the heart of the Valley.

But enough about the past. The Shenandoah is a valley of wonder, with historic downtowns, sweeping orchards and stunning natural features, all centered on the Shenandoah River. The word "Shenandoah" is a Native American term for "daughter of the stars."

STONEWALL JACKSON'S MILITARY SUCCESS MADE HIM A STAR of the CIVIL WAR

Q. Which Virginian was the first to fly an airplane over the North Pole?

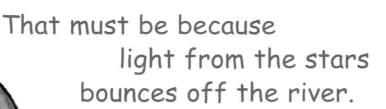

That must be because
light from the stars
bounces off the river.

You're pretty clever, Penny! With more than 90 apple orchards, Winchester is the "apple capital of the world." Farther south, you can walk through 64 acres of underground caves at the Luray Caverns. Some of the formations have been turned into pipes called the Great Stalactite Organ. *The Guinness Book of World Records* designated it as "the world's largest natural musical instrument." Then there is the Natural Bridge that the Monocan Indians called "Bridge of Gods." It is like a giant stone arc 215 feet high and 90 feet across. Jefferson was so impressed that he bought it and 157 surrounding acres. When Washington was a young surveyor, he carved his initials in the rock.

 Richard Evelyn Byrd, in 1926. His brother was Harry Flood Byrd, one of Virginia's most powerful governors.

Here we are at last at the end of our journey in western Virginia, where some of the friendliest Virginians live in the peace and quiet of the Allegheny Mountains. Today, it is a region of small towns where coal mining is one of the main ways to make money, but this was one of the hottest spots in the United States when our nation was but a pup. This is the site of the Cumberland Gap, the only natural break in the Appalachian Mountain range from Maine to Georgia that is easy to cross on foot. Large game animals, such as buffalo, went through the gap in migrations thousands of years ago. It was a major transportation route for Native Americans hunting game and on the warpath. When white

Q. Where was the soft drink, Dr Pepper created?

settlers arrived, it became the most important route on the western frontier. Daniel Boone and about 30 woodsmen carved a path through the Cumberland Gap called the Wilderness Road, which 200,000 to 300,000 white settlers used to cross into Kentucky and expand the United States westward. Today, Cumberland Gap is a national park. It is especially beautiful in the fall when the leaves change colors.

I had no idea Virginia had so many places to see, so many important people, and so much history and culture to learn about.

Well, every state in America has its own story to tell— and Virginia's is one of the most exciting of them all!

 In Rural Retreat, Virginia. The period after "Dr" had to be removed because the name does not refer to a legal physician.

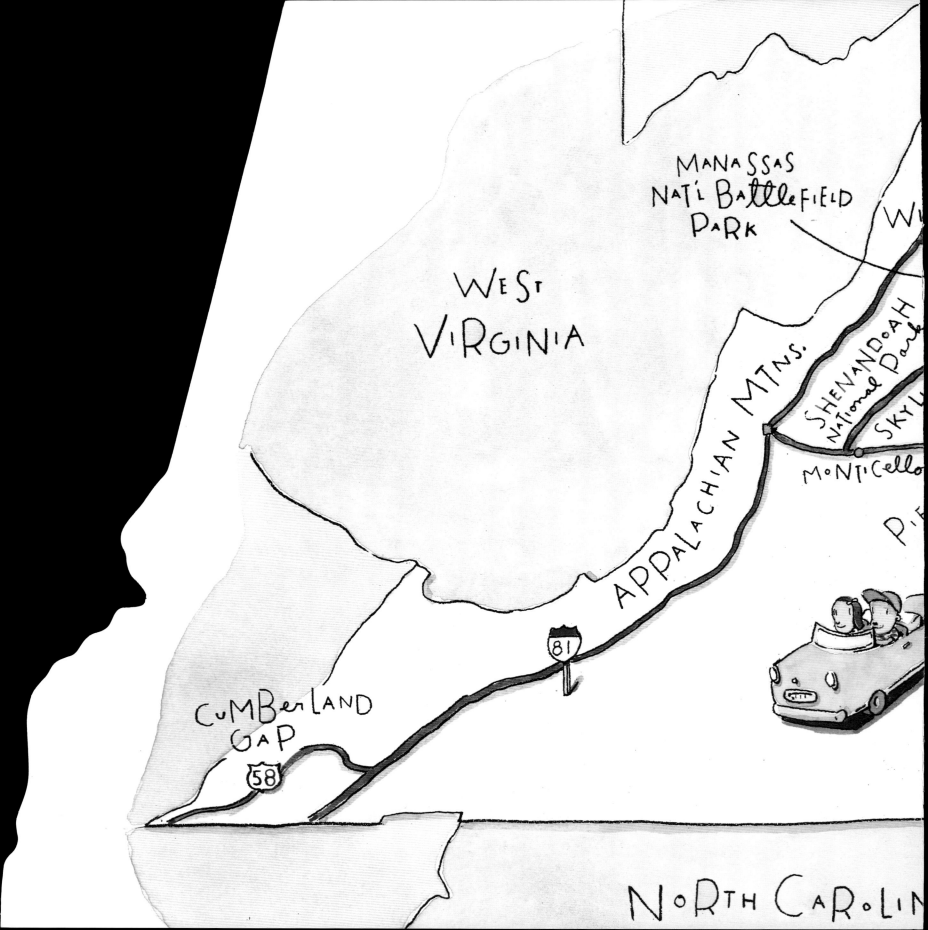

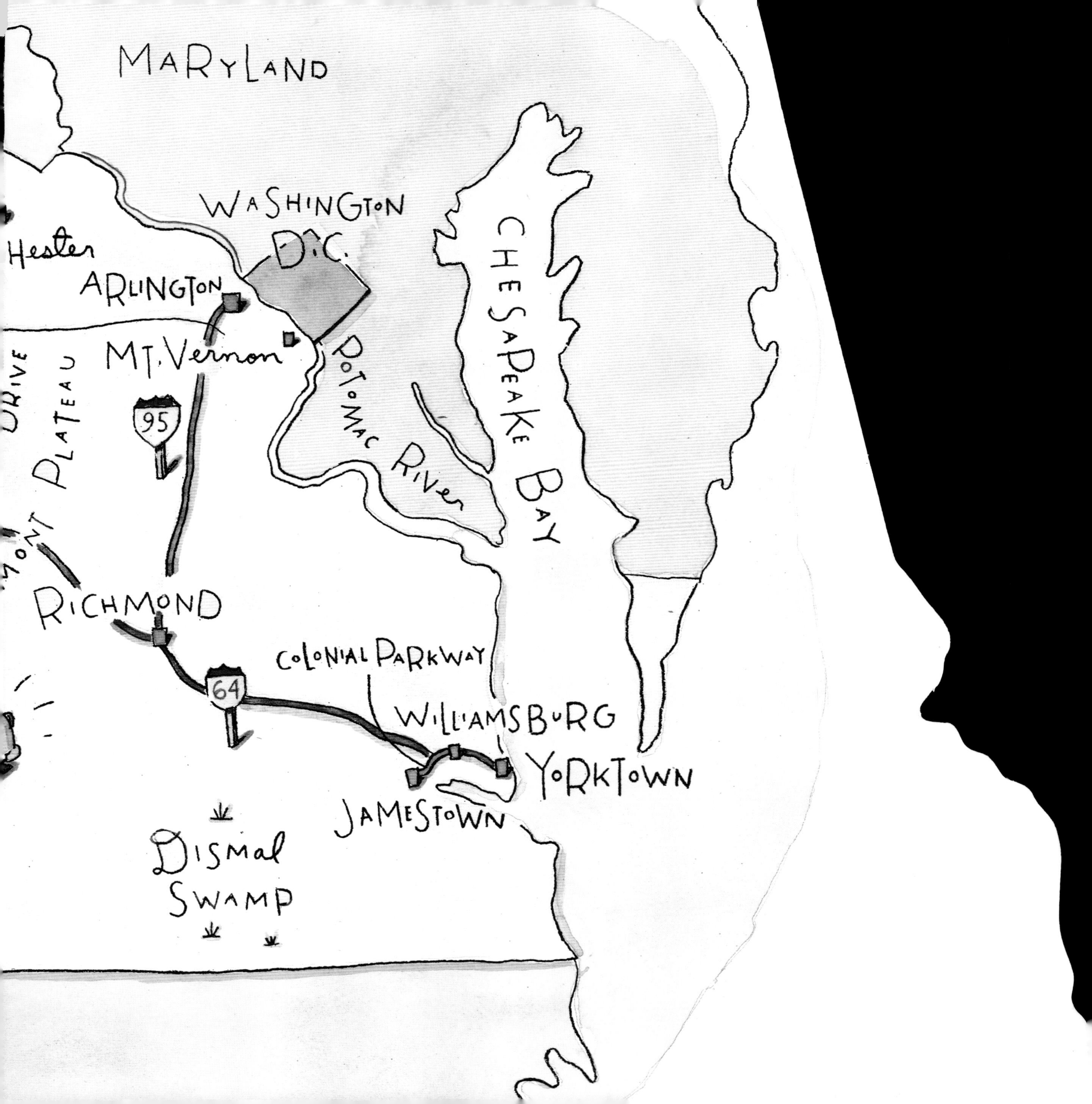
MARYLAND
WASHINGTON D.C.
Hester
ARLINGTON
MT. Vernon
DRIVE
PLATEAU
95
POTOMAC River
CHESAPEAKE BAY
MONT
RICHMOND
COLONIAL PARKWAY
64
WILLIAMSBURG
YORKTOWN
JAMESTOWN
Dismal SWAMP

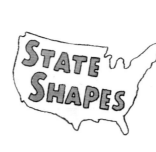